FINDING YOUR
Beebo

WRITTEN AND ILLUSTRATED BY
Uday Dandavate

Celebrating the arrival of our granddaughter.

Uday Dandavate, June 2021

ACKNOWLEDGEMENTS

I owe thanks to several people for this project. Anje Vogt, a facilitator of creativity in children, inspired me to take my poetry to children. The teachers of Washington Elementary School in Richmond, California, especially Mary Ann Lafosse and Nancy Pasqua, provided valuable feedback to my early version of the manuscript. Brandie Kasprzak, a substitute teacher at Mt. Lebanon School District in Pittsburgh, Pennsylvania also provided invaluable feedback to both the illustrations and the text in this book. She even invited her husband and children to provide their feedback.

I invited six children Quinn (8), Saddie (13), Drew (11), Howard (6), Coco (10), and Milan (8) to draw a picture of a character that represented the voice in their head. Beebo was inspired by a character drawn by 10 year old Coco from Michigan. My friend Jagruti Patel, family child care committee chair at CAAEYC, Redlands, CA, provided invaluable feedback for targeting appropriate age groups. Other parent friends, Melanie Solka, MacKinzie Shaw, Brianna Sylver, Tracey Lovejoy, Divya Adinarayanan, Sumitra Naganathan, Shalini Sarna, Sonia Tiwari, and Aimee Snow, were always there with timely feedback when I needed to make decisions about the illustrations or the message.

Molly Pearson as an editor of this book helped me to make my message clear and succinct. When I decided to write the book, I approached three of my friends, Norio Fujikawa and Bren Bataclan for illustration help, and Dr. Peter Chan for design help, with Cindy Kao for assisting him in the process. The three of them encouraged me to draw the illustrations myself. After an almost 20 year gap I was motivated to get back to drawing. I must have tried several hundred illustrations before settling on the final art in consultation with Norio, Peter, and Bren.

My immediate family, my wife Rohini, daughter Isha, son-in-law AJ, and my 90 year old mother-in-law Vijaya Doshi gave me feedback on almost every illustration I drew over the past nine months. Isha came up with the name Beebo.

Without all of your help Find your Beebo would not have been possible.
Thanks a lot for your contribution.

Finding Your Beebo

Contents

Where is Beebo?

Beebo is
the child inside you
your best friend

when you feel
confused
upset or
angry

you can talk to Beebo
and be understood

You can find Beebo
in your imagination
you can see Beebo
with your eyes closed
you can hear Beebo
in a quiet room

In Beebo
you will always
have a friend
when
you need one

when you feel happy
you can sing and dance
with Beebo

Beebo will never leave your side.

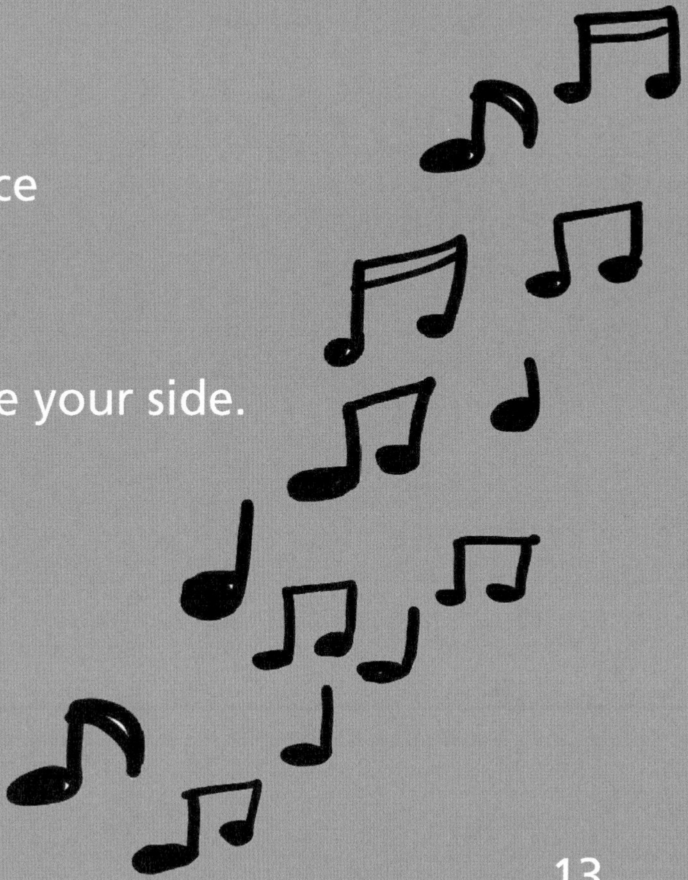

Talk to Beebo . . .

14

You can talk to Beebo
about your future

**imagine it
feel it
build it**

Imagine it

When someone or something
seems too far away
you can bring it closer
with your imagination

imagination
helps you bring
your dreams alive

when you see something
with your eyes closed
that's your imagination

your eyes
show you what is real
your imagination
shows you what is possible

when something seems
impossible or difficult
you need imagination
to make it possible.

Feel it

Close your eyes
and feel

what do you hear?
what do you smell?

remember how you feel...

when you are thirsty
and take a sip of water

when you see
your best friend smile

remember how you feel
when someone you love cries

that feeling
is called empathy

when you care for someone
you understand their feelings

by understanding feelings
you learn to care
to share
and to love.

Build it

To make music
you use
your hands
and your voice

to dance
you use
your whole body
and your feelings

to build something new
you use your experience
and your imagination

you can build anything
with your imagination
and practice

practice means
doing it over and over
until you gain mastery
remember
how many tries it takes
to gain mastery at
tying your shoelaces.

Beebo knows a lot about you . . .

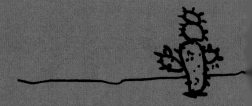

Beebo says
"the child inside of you
is so good at

**observing
listening
safe keeping
solving problems"**

you can use
your power.

Observing

To see
what's behind you
you turn around

to listen
to the sounds around you
you pay attention

to smell
the flowers beside you
you inhale your breath

to express love
you hug

when you observe
with your five senses

seeing
hearing
smelling
touching
tasting

you become
aware
of what life has to offer.

Listening

Ask why
and you will
learn something

ask again
and you will
learn even more

keep asking why
and you will
get to the truth

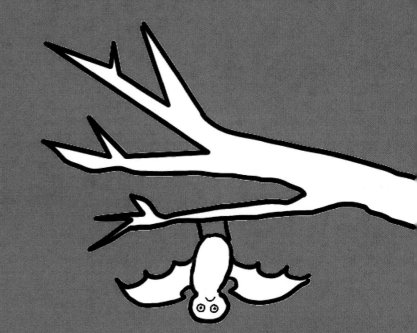

40

ask someone why
and you will learn
about them

ask yourself why
and you will learn
about yourself

ask mother nature why
and listen to her answers.

Safe keeping

When you care for others
others care for you

caring
feels warm and refreshing

it helps you unwind
untangle
and heal

caring for humans
is what water
is to plants

nourishment
and growth.

Solving problems

A problem
is not a dead end
it is a sign

that there is more
to discover
than what you
already know

solving one problem
makes you smarter

solving more problems
makes you wiser

48

a problem
is a chance

to know more
to learn more
to find a way forward

a problem
is a temporary obstacle
if you accept the challenge

it is a call
to consider
better options
and take action.

49

Beebo knows a few things
about life . . .

Beebo says growing up means learning to

live together
make space
connect the dots
enjoy diversity
look for more
respect nature
understand science

discover yourself.

53

Live together

Living together
helps a family
develop love

working together
we can make music
get new ideas
help each other

sharing stories
helps
build bonds
make friends
preserve traditions
grow a family
create hope

55

and above all
stories remind us
of who we are
and where we came from

living together
working together
we get strength to
move faster and farther

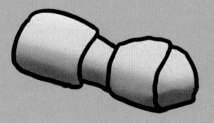

when we do something good
we need a pat on the back

when we make a mistake
we need someone to correct us

when we are lost
we need someone
to find us a way

above all
we need someone
who cares

together we can do more
than we can alone.

Make space

The sun
and the moon
are so different

the sun is hot
the moon is cold

they just can't
get along

but in the sky
there is a place
and there is a time
for both

when you make space
and make time
for someone
so different
it is called
consideration

when two people
are different
they can argue
and they can fight

or they can each
have their own
place and time

when you learn to
consider
you begin to
understand

when you learn to
understand
you begin to share

just like
the sun
and the moon.

Connect the dots

Stars in the sky
are shiny dots

together
they fill the sky with light

earth is made of
tiny grains

together
they keep a forest standing

drops of water
falling from the sky
are tiny dots
together
they bring us rain

ideas
in our head
are tiny dots

the stars in the sky
particles of earth
and raindrops

when they come together
they create a big idea

to design life
we need to collect small ideas
and turn them into
one big idea.

Enjoy diversity

Can you imagine
a rainbow with a single color
or music with no variation?

diversity gives us
choices of

colors
flavors
feelings
people

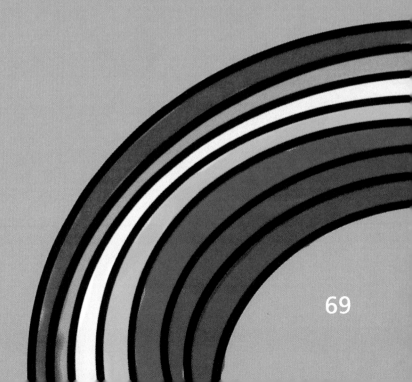

diversity gives us
inspiration

diversity is life.

Look for more

When you look at something
you can only see
what is
right in front of you

there is always
more
than what
your eyes can perceive

you must go behind your eyes
to see the other side

from where you sit
you can only see
where your eyes can reach

74

to know more
you can ask others
what they see
from where they sit

when you are able to look
from all sides
and know what others see
you will learn more
than what you can perceive
from where you sit.

Respect nature

If you smile at a dog
the dog smiles back at you

if you give love to a tree
the tree gives love back to you

if you nourish the earth
the earth nourishes you

if you feed the birds
the birds sing for you

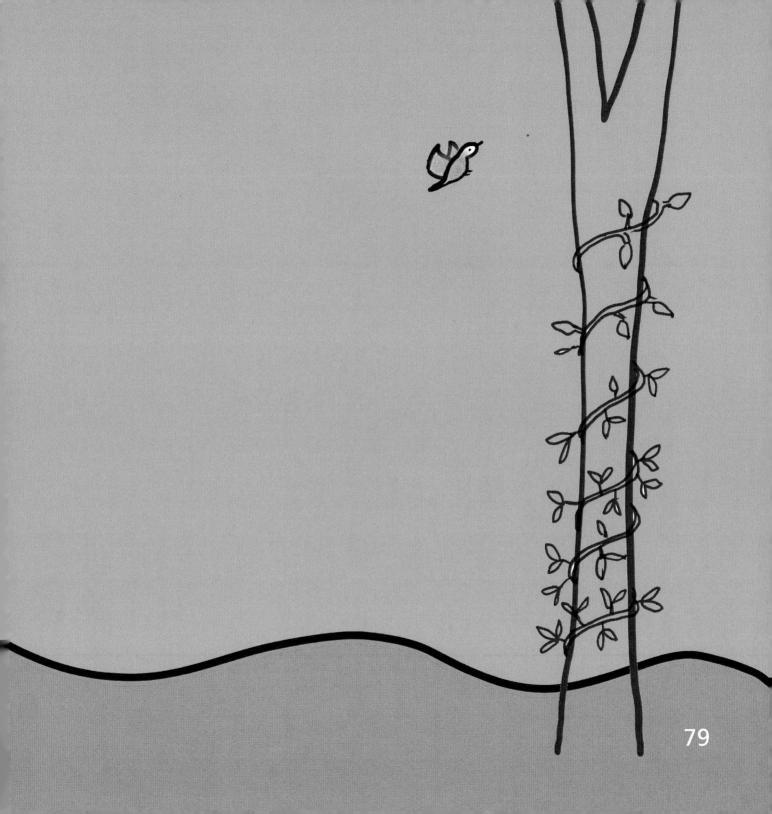

Understand science

When I was a a little kid
I wondered

why there was
day and night

where the rain came from
and where the clouds were
going

I wondered
why we could talk
and animals could not

as I looked at the ants
that disappeared
into the cracks
I wondered
how they live

I found my answers
when I learned that
there is a higher power
that keeps the world going

it's called nature

nature has set rules
for how everything works
we call that science

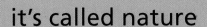

understanding science helps
design
create
and imagine
new objects into existence
that improve life

like electricity and microwaves
cars and airplanes
vaccines and medicines

and even though
I understand science a bit
I still wonder
where the ants go.

The only limit is you
what you can see
the dots you connect
the love you create
the future is yours to imagine.

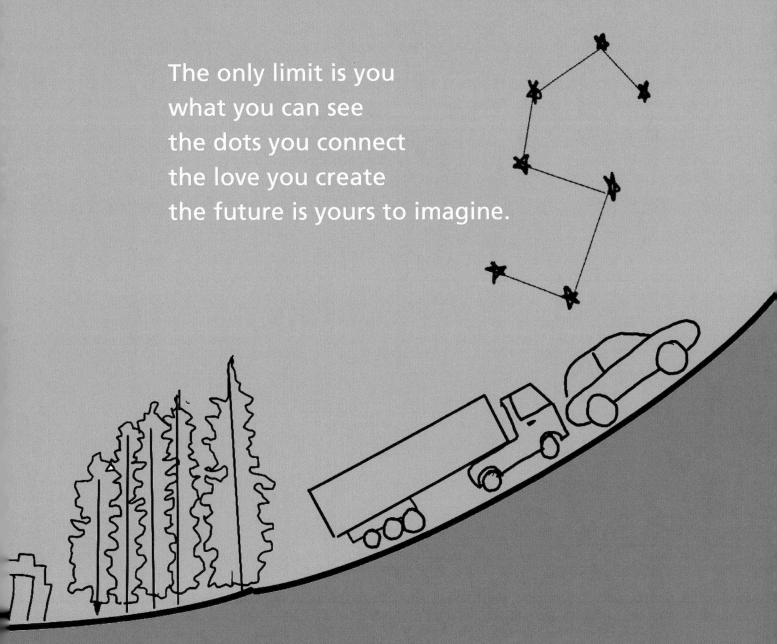

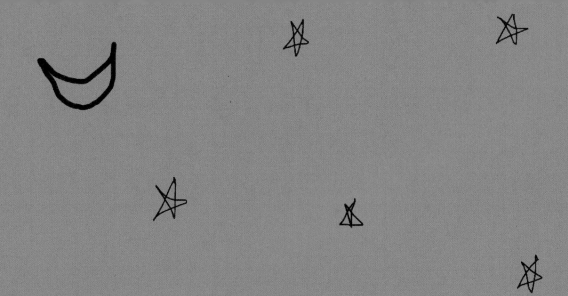

About the author . . .

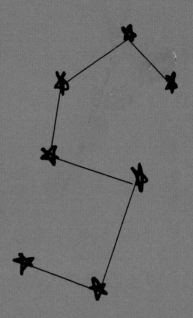

UDAY DANDAVATE

A design activist and ethnographer of social imagination,
Uday Dandavate is also CEO of SonicRim, a San Francisco based
design research company specializing in co-creation. He has traveled
extensively around the world, studying and connecting with all
kinds of people and cultures, and watching and participating
as they change over time. In his professional capacity he enjoys
blogging, teaching, speaking, and facilitating. Uday inspires fresh
perspectives that help to humanize technologies and democratize
design. Uday's mission is to cultivate curiosity, compassion, and
creativity in people of all ages and cultures.

Finding Your Beebo . . .

This is the end
of the book
and the beginning
of our friendship

even without this book
you can talk to me anytime
and ask me questions
or just express
how you are feeling
then close your eyes
and I'll be there for you
in your imagination

when you are feeling
confused
angry
upset or
bored
you can call me anytime

I promise that
when you grow up
I'll still be there for you

Finally,

We have intentionally left
some artwork in this book blank
so you can color Beebo
with the colors in your imagination.

On the next few pages
we have provided space for you
to write down your thoughts
or questions that you want to
discuss with Beebo.

When you find some quiet time,
you can talk to Beebo
in your imagination.

. . . .

. . . .

. . . .

. . . .

. . . .

. . . .

. . . .

. . . .

FINDING YOUR BEEBO

....

....

....

....

....

....

....

....

....

....

....

....

....

....

....

....

Finding Your Beebo

Author and Illustrator:
Uday Dandavate

Editor:
Molly Pearson

Art Director:
Peter Kwok Chan

Associate Designer:
Cindy Kao

Illustrators (Uday's Portrait on p.89):
Sandip Bajpeyi and Pravin Mishra

ISBN no: 9798509568633

Published in the United States in June 2021

Published by Kindle Direct Publishing

dandavate1@gmail.com

Made in the USA
Monee, IL
29 December 2022